a KALEIDOSCOPIA colorin

The Magical World of...
Ann's Doodles

Created by Ann Marie Irvine

Ann's Doodles; The Magical World of
Copyright 2015 Ann Marie Irvine

Dedicated to my dad

Published by Kaleidoscopia Coloring Books
Kaleidoscopia Coloring Books, 2205 California Street NE Suite #300, Minneapolis, MN 55418

Printed in the United States of America on Acid-free paper.

Visit KaleidoscopiaColoringBooks.com for our full selection of coloring books designed with you in mind.

KaleidoscopiaColoringBooks.com

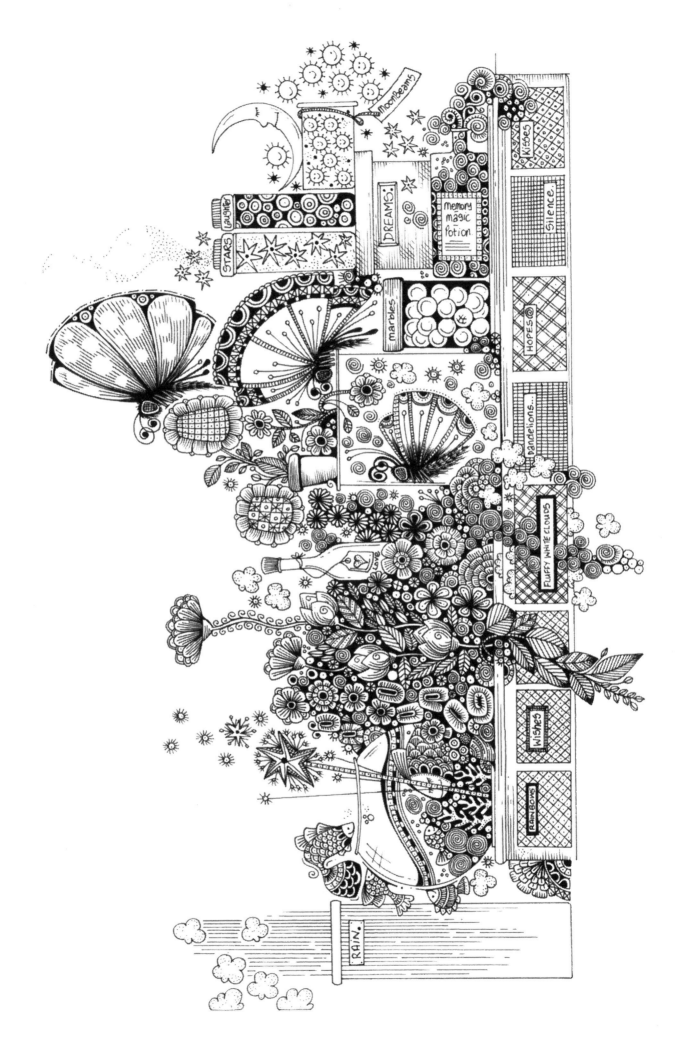

The Magical World of Ann's Doodles.... Drawing Titles

1. A Gift For A Butterfly
2. All For The Unicorn
3. As If By Magic
4. Beginnings
5. Bottle Collection
6. Bubbles
7. Butterfly Dream Jar
8. Butterfly Feast
9. Catch Your Dreams
10. Climb Rainbows To The Moon
11. Cuddle Up Bottle
12. Daisys And Leaves
13. Catch Your Dreams
14. Dreamer
15. EarlyBugs
16. FishFlutterbies And Flowers
17. Fish House
18. Flowery
19. FlyAway Fishes
20. Great Balloon Fix
21. Harold Matilda William
22. Jar Collection
23. King Of Cuddle Up Castle
24. Lean On Me
25. Let There Be
26. Little Bitty House
27. Moonicorn
28. More Spectacular Happenings
29. My Collection
30. Olivia
31. On The Moon
32. Puff The Magic Pony
33. Rainbow Juice
34. RainbowMaker
35. Rainbow Potion
36. Rosie
37. Happy Seahorse
38. Almost
39. Smiles All Around
40. Spectacular Happenings
41. Stronger Than You Look
42. Surprise
43. Teeny Tiny Tots
44. The Fish That Kissed Mr Moon
45. The Great Chocolate Drop
46. The Hedgehog And The Star
47. The Smiles
48. Tiny Little Fish
49. Up Up Away
50. We Can All Be Friends
51. Winds Of Change
52. The Magical Wonderland

Made in the USA
San Bernardino, CA
26 November 2016